A CRASH OF RHINOS
A PARTY OF JAYS

The Wacky Ways We Name Animal Groups

TEXT BY **Diane Swanson**
ILLUSTRATIONS BY **Mariko Ando Spencer**

 **annick press**
toronto + new york + vancouver

With their super sense of smell, bears really are **sleuths**. They sniff the air for signs of danger. And they follow clues to dinner: the scent of squirrels underground or the smell of seals beneath the snow.

SLEUTH OF BEARS

neat to know ➤

- The layers in a bear's teeth can show the animal's age.
- Polar bears even have fur on the soles of their feet.
- Grizzly bears sometimes hide leftovers and eat them later.

Pine processionary (pro-SESH-uhn-airy) caterpillars really form **ARMIES**. They camp down together, then file out for food. Traveling head to rump, the caterpillars march off to attack needles on trees, such as pines.

ARMY OF CATERPILLARS

neat to know

- Pine processionary caterpillars can make a line 12 meters (40 feet) long.
- Moving from their nests of silk and leaves, the caterpillars slip through holes the width of pencils.
- Poisonous bristles on their backs help protect the caterpillars.

Giant clams really rest in **BeDS**. They nestle in coral reefs with other warm-sea creatures. Some clams spin strong threads that help to hold them in place. The huge weight of others is enough to keep them in bed.

BeD OF CLamS

neat to know

- A giant clam is the largest clam in the world. It can weigh 230 kilograms (500 pounds).
- The giant clam's thick shells don't slam shut. They close very slowly.
- Plantlike algae live within giant clams, making food for themselves AND the clams.

In autumn, ducks called mallards really swim in **RAFTS**. The males cluster on water in ponds, lakes, and rivers. When a female mallard paddles among them, the males swim more closely together, grunting and whistling.

RAFT OF DUCKS

neat to know ➤

- Some mallard ducklings hatch high up in trees, then tumble down, damage-free.
- A mallard eats food left on its bill after pushing out the water it sucked in.
- By pretending to drink, male mallards show they're not going to attack.

- One elk guards against danger while the others rest.
- Elk can gallop, but they often just stroll.
- An elk can easily leap a fence that's taller than a door.

gang of elk

North American deer called elk, or wapiti (WAHP-uh-tee), really hang out in **gangs**. A male elk with a group of females might fight other males that try to take over. Heads bang and antlers clang when male elk battle.

Rising nearly as high as a two-story house, giraffes really **tower** above other animals. When they stretch to the top branches of trees, the giraffes stand especially tall. Then out comes a l-o-n-g tongue to grab leaves for lunch.

Tower of Giraffes

neat to know

- Giraffes are the tallest of all the animals on Earth.
- Each giraffe wears a coat with its own spotted pattern.
- Giraffes often sleep standing up.

Steller's jays really know how to **Party**. Noisy and bold, some hang upside down from eavestroughs on houses. Others perch near windows, peeking inside. And they eat almost anything – even tossed-out pizza or popcorn.

PARTY OF JAYS

neat to know

- To build nests of twigs and leaves, Steller's jays use mud.
- Steller's jays often hold food with their feet.
- By hammering with their beaks, Steller's jays crack open nuts.

Adult leopards really do **Leap**. In a single jump, they can bound 6 meters (20 feet). And they can spring 3 meters (10 feet) straight up. Mother leopards leap on prey when hunting food for their cubs as well as for themselves.

LeAP OF LeoPARDS

neat to know ➤

- Leopards are great swimmers. They seem to like water.
- Of all the big wild cats, leopards are the strongest climbers.
- Leopards eat many different kinds of animals – including beetles.

A male lion really seems to take **PRIDE** in himself. Called the "King of Beasts," he has no natural enemies. When he lives with female lions, they do much of the work. They care for the cubs and do most of the hunting.

PRIDE OF LIONS

neat to know

- A male lion weighs up to 250 kilograms (550 pounds).
- Female lions help one another raise their cubs.
- Working together, lions can hunt big animals such as African buffalo.

 neat to know

- Golden pheasants spend much of their time on the ground, but they rest in trees.
- A male golden pheasant is one of the world's most dazzling birds.
- The sun can fade the colors in a golden pheasant's feathers.

BOUQUET OF PHEASANTS

With their flashy colors and long feather tails, golden pheasants are showy birds. A male is so multicolored that he makes a **BOUQUET** all on his own. But put several males together and you have a really bright bouquet.

At mating times, male rhinos really can **CRASh**. If two males are fighting over a female rhinoceros, they might charge each other. Some try to bash their rivals with their horns. The battles can even be deadly.

CRASh OF RhinOS

neat to know →

- Rhinos have trouble seeing, but they hear and smell well.
- An Indian rhino's horn can be 60 centimeters (24 inches) long.
- A black rhino uses its upper lip to snatch leaves from trees.

Annick Press Ltd.

Edited by Elizabeth McLean
Cover design and interior design by Daniel Choi and Maggie Woo/Daniel Choi Design

Cataloging in Publication
Swanson, Diane, 1944—
    A crash of rhinos, a party of jays : the wacky ways we name animal
groups / by Diane Swanson ; illustrated by Mariko Ando Spencer.

ISBN-13: 978-1-55451-048-1 (bound)
ISBN-10: 1-55451-048-1 (bound)
ISBN-13: 978-1-55451-047-4 (pbk.)
ISBN-10: 1-55451-047-3 (pbk.)

    1. Animal societies—Juvenile literature. 2. Social behavior in
animals—Juvenile literature. 3. Animals—Terminology—Juvenile literature.
I. Spencer, Mariko Ando II. Title.
QL775.S94 2006   j591.56   C2006-900810-8

The text was typeset in Petit Latin and Cheri.
The art was rendered in watercolor.

We acknowledge the support of the Canada Council for the Arts, the Ontario Arts Council, and the Government
of Canada through the Book Publishing Industry Development Program (BPIDP) for our publishing activities.

Printed and bound in China.

Published in the U.S.A. by   **Distributed in Canada by:**   **Distributed in the U.S.A. by:**
Annick Press (U.S.) Ltd.   Firefly Books Ltd.   Firefly Books (U.S.) Inc.
                                 66 Leek Crescent   P.O. Box 1338
                                 Richmond Hill, ON   Ellicott Station
                                 L4B 1H1   Buffalo, NY 14205

Visit our website at: **www.annickpress.com**